AF229852

THE USURY DEBT TRAP

SULAIMAN ABDUL ALEEM

ISBN NUMBER FOR BOOK IN
PAPERBACK
 978-1-64945-049-4

ISBN NUMBER FOR EBOOK
ISBN 978-1-64945-050-0

THE REMAINDER IS PUBLISHER PAGE

+

ABOUT THE AUTHOR

Sulaiman Abdul Aleem, is a graduate of Chicago State University where he received a Master's Degree in Curriculum and Instruction with a concentration in Adult Education. He was a lecturer at the Sudan University of Science and Technology in

4

Khartoum in the 1990's. He also has written multiple articles for Islamic Publications.

The cover is a depiction of the current benefactors of usury. Driven by greed, their flag is the dollar.

ACKNOWLEDGEMENT
I would like to thank Asiya, whose tireless efforts and Jolie (cover illustrator) who helped to make this book possible.

*

TABLE OF CONTENTS

Page

-INTRODUCTION-

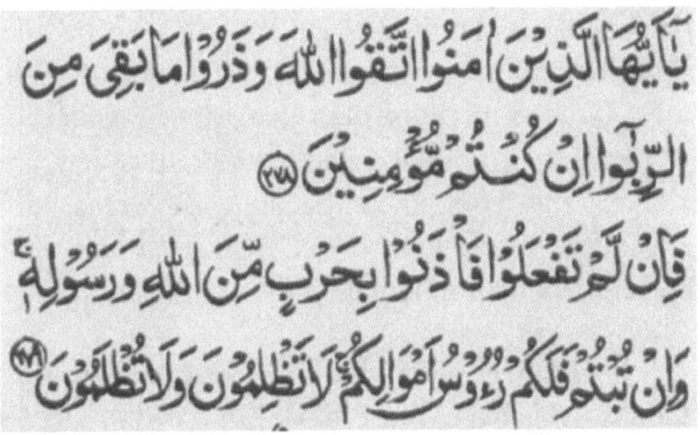

O you who believe! Fear Allah, and give up what remains of your demand for usury, If you are indeed believers. If you do not, take notice of war from Allah and his Messenger: But if you repent you shall have your capital sums: deal not unjustly, and you shall not be dealt with unjustly.

Quran 2(al Bakarah):278-279.

One scholar believes this is only refers to the hereafter, but when you see who benefits from all the financial boom and bust periods only one group stands out, the money lenders. The goldsmiths are the forefathers of the money lenders because people would leave their money with them on account of their secure safes. Goldsmiths observed that when people wanted to withdraw their gold, they never took all of it at once. The amount that remained became the reserve of the goldsmiths to be loaned out, with a certain amount of discretion. This immediately expanded their pot.

Today's schoolbooks generally portray the Middle Ages as a time of economic slavery, backwardness, and economic servitude, from which the only salvation for people were the Industrial Revolution. Some historians painted a quite different picture. A laborer could provide all the necessities for his family for a year by only working 14 weeks. Fourteen weeks is only a quarter of a year! The rest of the time, some men worked for themselves, some studied, or fished. Some helped build the Cathedrals that appeared all over Europe. During that period massive works of art were built, mainly, with volunteer labor. All of this was possible before the onslaught of usury.

MONEY CREATION THROUGH DEBTS

In the chase of profits through interest banks are free to create money as the current global currencies are all flat. Because the global currencies are not backed up by Gold or any precious metals, they have no intrinsic value. There is nothing to stop the perpetual printing of money. The U.S. has used $1.3 trillion in notes and coins to lend over $11 trillion worldwide. This side of the economy is valued more than the real economy since the size of the worldwide bond market is estimated at $45 trillion. The size of the world's stock market is estimated at $51 trillion. The world derivatives market has been estimated at $480 trillion, more than 30 times the size of the U.S. economy and 12 times the size of the economy of the entire world. Essential to understanding these events is that all money in the banking system has been created out of nothing through the process of making loans. The FDIC is not insurance, because the presence of "moral hazard" makes the thing it supposedly protects against more likely to happen. The final cost of the bailout, therefore is transferred to the public in the form of a hidden tax called *inflation*.

All of the money to achieve these bailouts was made possible by the Federal Reserve System acting as the "lender of last resort." That was one of the motives for which it had been created. We must not forget that the phrase "lender of last resort" means that the money is created out of nothing, resulting in the confiscating of our nation's wealth through the hidden tax called *inflation*.

The current monetary scheme is a "cruel hoax". The hoax is that there is no real money in the system, only debts. Except for coins, which are issued by the government and make up only one-thousandth of the money supply, the entire U.S. money supply consist of debt to private banks. This is a result of money *they created* with accounting entries on their books.

FRACTIONAL RESERVE SYSTEM

It was Goldsmiths who developed fractional reserve banking as they realized the gold deposited with them was never all withdrawn at any given time, they began the process of lending more money than they had in their possession. This was achieved by issuing bills which promised gold on demand. As long as loans were not due at the same time and long as depositors did not withdraw all their deposits at any given time then this illusion would produce handsome rewards for the Goldsmiths, who are the forefathers of today's bankers. This shows that actual money which has been given in debt by the banking industry does not exist.

Fractional reserve banking creates illusionary money, which actually led to the explosive growth in the U.S. sub-prime sector and the wider economy. Because such factors are not real, confidence changes daily. This is what causes the sharp rise and falls in the financial markets. Because the public's pensions, bonds, deposits and interest rates are based on the performance of the markets this causes consistent uncertainty and instability. The net effect is that a negative effect on the financial markets and banking will inevitability have an effect in the real economy. To compensate for these expectations, companies will adjust their spending, investment and recruiting strategies according to what they expect to occur in the economy in the coming years. If they are expecting a collapse or significant downturn, they will spend less. As more companies do this, we get a vicious circle of less spending, higher unemployment and eventually a recession.

The moral hazard from this arises because banks do not bear the full consequences of their actions and act more irresponsible than they otherwise would have if not insulated from risk. The sub-prime sector preyed on the weak, who have no means to buy a house. They were lent money at very high interest rates and when the sector turned sour central banks pumped in billions of dollars to shore up banks that made unscrupulous loans.

Precious metals were the first commodity money to appear in history and ever since have been proven by actual experience to be the only reliable base for an honest monetary system. Gold, as the basis of money, can take several forms: bullion, coins, and fully backed paper receipts. Man has been plagued throughout history with the falsehood that the quantity of money is important, specifically that more money is better than less. This has led to perpetual manipulation and expansion of the money. During one period when the Bank of England pressured the colonies to abandon their fiat money, general prosperity quickly returned. The supply through such practices as coin clipping, debasement of the coin content, and, in latter centuries, the issuance of more paper receipts than there was gold to back them. In every case, these applications have led to economic and political disaster. In these rare instances where man has refrained from controlling the money supply and has allowed it to be determined by free-market production of the gold supply, the result has been prosperity and tranquility.

Fiat money is paper money without precious metal backing which people by law are compelled to accept. During one period when the Bank of England forced the colonies to abandon their fiat money, general prosperity quickly returned. Fractional money always declines into pure fiat money.

When money is created out of nothing, the true interest rate is not 8% or 9% or even 22%. It is infinity. It is easier than printing and, because the process is not understood by the public, it is politically safe. Who cares if the scheme is damaging? Here is the perfect tool for obtaining unlimited funding for politicians and endless profits for bankers. And best of all, the little people who pay the bills for both groups have no idea what is being done to them. They began lending out pieces of paper that said they were receipts, but which in fact were *counterfeit*. The public could not tell one from the other and accepted both of them as money. From that point forward, the receipts in distribution exceeded the gold held in reserve, and the age of fractional-reserve banking had dawned. This led immediately to what would become an almost unbroken record to then to the present: a record of inflation, booms and busts, suspension of payments, bank failures, repudiation of currencies, and reappearing spasms of economic chaos.

The Bank of England was formed in 1694 by the Rothschilds to institutionalize fractional-reserve banking. As the world's first central bank, it initiated the concept of a partnership between bankers and politicians. The politicians would be given spendable money (created out of nothing by the bankers) without having to raise taxes. In return, the bankers would receive a commission on the transaction, deceptively called interest, which would continue constantly.

The American dollar has no intrinsic value. It is the classic example of fiat money with no limit to the quantity that can be manufactured. Its primary value lies in the willingness of people to receive it and, to that end, legal tender laws require them to do so. It is true that our money is created out of nothing, but it is more accurate to say that it is based on *debt*. In one sense, therefore, our money is created out of less than nothing. The entire money system would vanish into bank vaults and computer chips if all debts were settled up. Under the present system, therefore, our leaders cannot allow a serious reduction in either the consumer or national debt. Charging interest on pretended loans is usury, and that has become institutionalized under the Federal Reserve System. The Slight-of Hand Mechanism by which the Feds converts debt into money may seem complicated at first, but it is simple if one bears in mind that the process is not intended to be logical but confuse and deceive. The end product of the Slight-of-Hand Mechanism is artificial expansion of the money supply, which is the root cause of the hidden tax called inflation. This expansion then leads to contraction and, together, they produce the devastating boom-bust cycle that has plagued mankind throughout history wherever fiat money has existed. Who were these "subjects of a foreign power" who owned the bank? In <u>The History of the Great American Fortunes</u>, published in 1936, Gustavus Myers pointed to the powerful British banking dynasty of the House of Rothschild. Myers wrote:

> Under the surface, the Rothschilds long had a powerful influence in dictating American financial laws. The law records show that they were the power in the old Bank of the United States.

> Like the German Hanoverian kings, the Rothschild banking empire was British only in the perception that it had been in England for a long time.

Its roots were actually in Germany. The House of Rothschild was founded in Frankfort in the mid-eighteenth century, when a money lender named Mayer Amschel Bauer changed his name to Amschel Rothschild and fathered ten children. His five sons were sent to major capitals in Europe to open branches of the family business. Nathan, the shrewdest of these sons, went to London, where he opened the family branch called N. M. Rothschild & Sons. Nathan's brothers managed N. M. Rothschild's branches in Paris, Vienna, Berlin and Naples.

The family fortunes got a major increase in 1815, when Nathan pulled off the mother of all insider trades. He led British investors to believe that the Duke of Wellington had lost to Napoleon at the Battle of Waterloo. In a matter of hours, British government bond prices plunged. Nathan, who had advance information, swiftly bought up the entire market in government bonds acquiring a dominant holding in England's debt for pennies on the pound. Over the course of the nineteenth century, N. M. Rothschild would become the biggest bank in the world, and the five brothers would come to control most of the foreign-loan business in Europe. "Let me issue and control a nation's money," Nathan Rothschild boasted in 1838," and I care not who writes the laws."

DEBT ENSLAVEMENT

You can enslave a nation by one of two ways. One by military domination and the other by debt.

Servitude militarily, has the disadvantage that the slaves are likely to rebel. A continual force is necessary to keep them obedient. Servitude by debt can occur so silently that the slaves do not even know that they have new masters. American chattel slavery was viewed as inefficient by the British because you had to feed the slaves. Under economic slavery you make the slaves responsible for feeding themselves.

That new home has blinded Americans to their new masters. If the house attached to the driveway has a mortgage of around $250,000 at approximately 10% over a period of 25 years. They will pay for the house about three times. That means, in the time it took them to earn a half million dollars, someone is living off their sweat. Every payroll check that they receive is reduced by approximately 20% for the payment of federal income tax. The federal income tax was instituted

18

specifically to coerce taxpayers to pay the interest due the banks on the federal debt.

In an era of deception, the truth will always be radical. *Upton Sinclair*

SMOKE AND MIRRORS

The supposable justification for allowing lenders to charge whatever interest the market will bear is that it recognizes the time value. Lenders are said to be entitled to this fee in return for withholding the use of their money for a period of time. That argument might have some merit if the lenders were actually lending their own money. But in the case of credit card and other commercial bank debt, they aren't. *They aren't even lending their own money. They are lending nothing but the borrower's own credit.*

Of course, banks do not really pay out loans from the money they receive as deposits. If they did this, no additional money would be created. *What they do when they make loans is accept promissory notes in exchange for credits to the borrower's transactions accounts.*

19

Loans (assets) and deposits (liabilities) both rise by the same amount.

Here is how the credit card scheme works. When you sign a merchant's credit card slip, you are creating a "negotiable instrument." A negotiable instrument is anything that is signed and convertible into money or that can be used as money. The merchant takes this negotiable instrument and deposits it into merchant's checking account, a special account required of all business that accept credit. The account goes up by the amount on the slip, indicating that the merchant has been paid. The charge slip is forwarded to the credit card company (Visa, Mastercard, etc.), which bundles your charges and sends them to a bank. The bank then sends you a statement, which you pay with a check, causing your transaction account to be debited at your bank. **At no point has a bank lent you its money or its depositor's money**. Rather, your charge slip (a negotiable instrument) has become an "asset" against which credit has been advanced. Your bank has done nothing but monetize your own I.O.U. or promise to repay. The bank turns your promise to pay into an asset and liability at the same time, balancing its books without actually transferring any pre-existing money to you.

To eliminate some of the wiggle room for the consumers, the 2005 bankruptcy law was written by and for credit card companies. Credit card debt reached $735 billion by 2003, more than 11 times the tab in 1980. Approximately 60 percent of credit card users do not pay off their monthly balances, and among those users, the average debt carried on those cards is close to $12,000. *This subprime market is actually targeted by banks credit card companies,* which count on the working poor and the financially strapped to not be able to make their payments.

More than 75 percent of credit card profits come from people who make those low, minimum monthly payments. And who make monthly payments of 26 percent interest? Who pays late fees, over-balance charges, and cash advance premiums? Families that can barely make ends meet, households precariously balanced between financial survival and complete collapse. These are the families that are singled out by the lending industry, barraged with special offers, personalized advertisements, and home phone calls, all with one objective in mind: get them to borrow more money.

"Payday" lender operations offering small "paycheck advance" loans have mushroomed. Particularly popular in poor and minority communities, they can carry usurious interest rates as high as 500 percent. The debt crisis has been blamed on the imprudent spending habits of people buying frivolous things, but observations show that two-income families are actually spending 21 percent less on food, and 44 percent less on clothing and 40 percent less on appliances than one-income families spent a generation earlier. The reason is that they are spending substantially *more* on soaring prices and medical costs.

In 2003, the average family was spending 69 percent more on home mortgage payments in inflation-adjusted dollars than their parents spent a generation earlier, and 61 percent more on health needs. At the same time, real wages had stagnated and declined. Most people were struggling to get by with less; and in order to get by, many turned to credit cards to pay for basic necessities. Credit card companies and their affiliated banks capitalize on the extremity of poor and working-class people by using high pressure tactics to sign up borrowers they know can't afford their loans then jacking up interest rates or forcing customers to buy "insurance" on the loans. People who can only make minimal payments on their credit card bills windup being "sharecroppers" to the banks.

The Economic Policy Institute reports that, since 1972, the median hourly wage has remained basically flat, and has actually declined for the bottom fifth of workers. Women saw more of an improvement, but that's because women were grossly underpaid in 1972. What is more astonishing is that in this very same period, when workers were losing financial ground, their productivity (their output per hour) had nearly *doubled.* They were doing twice as much work for the same wage or less. In fact, the U.S. minimum wage, adjusted for inflation, has never regained its 1968 value. Fully 47 percent of Americans now report living from paycheck to paycheck.

People supplemented this financial reality by going into debt. You may object: "Why did people have to go into debt? After all family income went up." That's true, but only because more family members are working. The income "gain" was an illusion. The more hours a couple or individual had to work the more they had to outsource their personal lives with day care, fast food and auto expenses (maintenance, insurance, registration) etc. The longer we are away from home, the less we take home at the end of the day.

MODERN DAY SHARECROPPING

The growing gap between how much we produced and how much we earned led to a bizarre paradox. As the economy grew, individual people became worse off. Even people who were making more money were living in a way that put them deeper in debt. This gap creates an environment where people are driven into servitude.

This twenty-first century sharecropping is called payday lending. Each commitment under it begins, fittingly, with a bad check. Like a sharecropping contract, a payday loan essentially becomes a lien against your life, entitling the creditor to a share of your future earnings indefinitely. With payday lending, the "debt trap" is not a figure of speech. The loan is actually structured as a trap. Once caught in the cycle, the borrower faces a choice each payday---pay Check Into Cash $30 (to rollover the loan) or pay Check Into Cash $230 on a $300 loan.

Government studies show that in North Carolina regulators (who made payday loans illegal) found that 87% of borrower's rollover their loans. Indiana found that approximately 77% of its payday loans were rollovers. This is hardly surprising, of course, if your finances are so busted that a doctor visit or a car repair puts you in the red, chances are slim that you will be able to pay back an entire loan plus interest a few days after taking it out.

The marketing company Nielsen Claritas breaks down American consumers into dozens of niche markets. They say the Check into Cash's target are in demographic #44, "Homespun Families," which forms a subset of the larger "Mass Middle Class" category. A disproportionate number of Clarita's 44s work in manufacturing, construction, or transportation. Jobs like factory worker, auto mechanic, and truck drivers are concentrated in Appalachia, the Deep South and Midwest Heartland.

As the Community Financial Services Association, the payday-lending industry's trade and lobbying group in Washington, puts it, "payday advance customers represent the heart of America's middle class". A terrifyingly accurate statement that testifies to the financial stability of all but the most affluent Americans. Unlike with check cashing, the market for payday loans is not the underclass. The 28 million Americans that have no bank account (a number that includes 20% of African-Americans and Latinos) don't have the checkbook with which to write the *bad* check. Millions more are ineligible for payday loans because they're unemployed or are paid off the books.

These are people who, despite flat incomes keep buying bigger houses through the infamous "liar loans." The payday loan too is a liar loan of sorts, though the relevant lie is not told to the banker or mortgage broker but to you. The lie is that you're still making it, you've hit a brief rough patch, and everything will work itself out soon.

DONALD TRUMP'S ADMINISTRATION

Over the past half-century, consumer protections have been whittled away, reorganized, or just poorly formulated. This results in a system in which the few are taking obscene wealth from the daily necessities of the many.

That same dynamic has been replicated in the public sector, where fees, such as parking tickets can easily increase with late fees and impound fees, now account for the vast bulk of government-revenue growth.

A very small percentage of Americans actually take out a payday loan, so it seems sort of marginal. But it is really a signifier of the structural problems of the American economy. The rise of payday lending was the most ubiquitous free-market response to the multigenerational crisis of wage stagnation. The payday loan is exactly what it says it is. You need a paycheck to get a payday loan.

A fee is anything that exceeds beyond the principle of a financial product. We have loan origination-fees, activation fees that you might get with a cell phone or Internet account. Particularly with payday lending, the industry uses this type of shell game, calling them fees and not interest, in order to circumvent state usury laws.

Over the last generation or two, we've seen that 80 to 90 percent of all new government-revenue growth has been the product of not taxation but of things like fees and fines. It's even more regressive than a flat tax.

We see the rise of fees increasingly targeting people of color, the fastest growing segment of Americans. Just because they are the most at risk doesn't mean they are the poorest. The middle class is becoming browner. Those are the people predatory lenders are eager to bring in because they have things like equity in their houses. They want people with assets.

Last November Richard Cordray, (former director of The Consumer Financial Protection Bureau) retired to run for governor of Ohio. His directorship was slated to end in July 2018. Trump's choice for his replacement was former House member Mick Mulvaney (R—SC), who immediately brought the bureau under the president's direct political control, charging appointees to trail career staffers in each CFPB division, moving critical supervisory and enforcement functions into the director's office, and appealing for no money for bureau operations at all. In June he sacked his entire advisory board after several members criticized his leadership during which time the name was changed to the Bureau of Consumer Financial Protection.

Among Mulvaney's more extreme moves has been to take the CFPB's bite out of student loans. American students are deeply in debt: 44 million owed a combined $1.5 trillion. Eight million are now currently in default, while 3 million more are at least two payments behind; three times as many people defaulted on student debt in 2016 than lost a home to foreclosure. That makes these borrowers impressionable to scams. Under Cordray, the bureau received 60,000 complaints through August 2017.That's one criticism per hour, 24 hours per day, 7 days a week. The CFPB was responsible for returning $750 million to injured borrowers, while conducting proactive supervision.

That didn't sit well with lenders, and Trump's new guard quickly moved to placate them. Even before Corday resigned, the Education Department bound the CFPB by saying it would stop portioning out student loan data with the "overreaching and unaccountable "agency". Upon his appointment Mulvaney collapsed the bureau's student-loan division into a consumer-education office a clear indication that the CFPB would focus on providing information about the loans, not on monitoring bad actors.

Seth Frotman tied the CFPB in 2016. Frotman was one of the highest-ranking federal officials overseeing student-loan servicers. By August of this year, he'd had enough: "You have used the bureau to serve the wishes of the most powerful financial companies in America," Frotman wrote in his incendiary resignation letter, noting that Mulvany's political appointees had "repeatedly undercut and weakened career CFPB staff" at the expense of students and to the great advantage of lenders. Frotman further alleged that the bureau's political staffers had cracked down on evidence that the nation's largest banks were "saddling (students) with legally dubious account fees."

If Frotman is right, this could have consequences on a massive civil action previously filed by the CFPB against Navient, the largest student-loan servicer in the country. Navient is accused of systematically deceiving borrowers about repayment options. In July, a judge turned down the company's motion to have the civil action discharged. Mulvany hasn't said whether the CFPB will proceed with the suit, but conservative editorial boards are urging him to ditch it. "What this means is that there are college kids out there who are being charged illegal fees by major banks." And the Trump administration's political staff that is in control of the bureau covered up that information."

Cynics might expect Trump to throw students under the bus. This is, after all, a president who paid a multimillion-dollar fraud case related to his own for-profit college. Less predictable, but equally disheartening, is the administration's handling of people in the armed forces.

Members of the military and veterans are uniquely vulnerable to loan sharks and scams. Roughly half of the United States' active-duty service members are under 25, and the military delivers many of them with their first regular paycheck. Young soldiers, sailors, and Air Force personnel with little credit histories are often required to move frequently around the country and overseas, sometimes with little announcement, so their spouses' scuffle to find stable work. In military towns with a high population of young people far from home and in need of credit, financial predators (particularly payday lenders and automobile financing firms) are eager to swoop in. The Defense Department has found that service members are four times as likely as civilians to be targeted by unscrupulous lenders.

To limit the damage, Congress passed the Military Lending Act of 2006, which put a ceiling on interest rates and extra charges, until recently the CFPB sanctioned some lenders who violated the act. But the bureau's work in this area seems unlikely to continue. Public records show that on August 2, representatives from the National Automobile Dealers Association met with officials from the Department of Defense and Mulvaney's Office of Management and Budget to discuss "Military Lending Act limitations on terms of consumer credit offered to service members and dependents." Documents indicate that the groups wanted relief from a rule restricting the sale of a type of insurance, called "guaranteed acceptance protection insurance "or GAP, to service members financing their cars with MLA-protected loans.

Automobile dealers like GAP insurance because it can be more beneficial than the sale of the car itself. They portray it as a common sense product that protects borrowers who owe more than what their car is worth if the vehicle gets stolen or totaled. But consumer advocates say GAP is a costly scam. A recent report from the National Consumer Law Center found that it was the second most frequently assertive add-on by car dealers, after service contracts. Markups on the insurance averaged 170 percent and that "consumers often find that GAP products fail to provide the promised benefits."

Representatives of the nation's car dealers and financiers present at the August 2 meeting wanted permission to keep pushing GAP on members of the military, according to records. What they got were no more cops on their beat. *The New York Times* reported a week later that the CFPB would stop proactively supervising these dealers and lenders. Paul Kantwill, a former Army colonel who joined the CFPB under Cordray in late 2016 as assistant director of servicemember affairs, likens this to "removing your sentries from the guard towers on your installation." Kantwill, who left the agency this past summer, cautions that "you may have the guard tower there, but if there is no one there to look at the fence line and to maintain surveillance, you can expect that bad performers are going to get in."

Among these bad performers is the Security National Automotive Acceptance Company, an Ohio-based business with expertise in auto loans to service members. Thanks to CFPB's oversight, we know that SNAAC has been cruel. When service members missed a loan payment, the company pursued them with bogus threats, according to an administrative order that the CFPB filed against SNAAC in 2015. SNAAC's debt collectors would also threaten service members with demotions or even discharges and resort to a loss of a security clearances or a potential demotion. After a sailor near Norfolk Naval Station in Virginia fell behind on car payments as a result of a divorce, SNAAC collectors "began to call and threaten me over the phone to include notifying my commanding officers." According to a 2015 complaint, the sailor gave up the car and eventually settled the debt. But a few years later, collectors suddenly "started calling me and intimidating me again."

The debt, somehow reappeared on credit reports as unresolved.

Whether this was done out of greed or sheer incompetence, it shows how necessary a watchdog like CFPB still is. The Defense Department can't protect its employees from this type of exploitation because it is not a financial regulator, and is a nonbank lender, a company like SNAAC would have operated with virtually no regulatory oversight if not for CFPB.

In 2015, the bureau filed an administrative order against SNAAC for unlawful debt-collection practices, forcing the company to return $2.28 million to service members and other borrowers and pay a $1 million penalty. The CFPB also obtained a separate court order banning SNAAC's practice of using overstating, deception and threats to compel payments from service members.

Kantwill says that the CFPB's newly inactive method means it will have to sit back and stand by on the SNAAC's of the world to victimize on service members; nothing will alter until consumers have been harmed. For members of the military, "it might mean that their careers have been undermined---and perhaps their family situations have been undermined as well."

The situation also poses a national-security danger. The Defense Department has found that financial turmoil has a demonstrable effect on military readiness and morale. Kantwill says he's seen it happen: "There is a direct correlation between financial enthusiasm and mission enthusiasm."

You think car dealers are filthy? It gets worse. Perhaps no other group has profited more directly from Mulvaney's neglect than payday lenders. Mulvaney's has transferred the CFPB's Office of Fair Lending and Equal Opportunity from the specialized Supervision, Enforcement and Fair Lending Division to the director's office. He also abandoned a suite against some of the most misleading creditors in the country like Golden Valley Lending, Silver Cloud Financial, Mountain Summit Financial, and Majestic Lake Financial.

Between August and December 2013, Golden Valley Lending and Silver Cloud Financial increased $27 million in payday loans and transgressed the Truth in Lending Act by hiding the true cost of these loans from consumers. According to CFPB complaint filed last year, these loans carried a guaranteed interest rates of 450 to 900 percent, meaning that a customer would have to pay up to $900 in interest alone over the course of a year on a $100 loan. By contrast, earlier this year the New York attorney general arrested 10 people connected to the Lucchese crime family for running a lucrative loan-sharking operation. The yearly rate of their "usurious loan payments "was 200 percent". It makes you wonder how the payday lenders escaped criminal charges.

But there was a snag. Though Golden Valley had simply contravened state usury laws, they contended to be protected by tribal sovereign protection, since they had incorporated on Indian reservations. This kept state authorities at bay, because they had no jurisdiction. But sovereign immunity cannot be invoked against the federal government, and the CFPB took the opportunity to step in.

When Mulvaney dropped the suit, he asserted the career staffers stood by his decision, only to retreat when NPR reported that his "entire career enforcement staff were against it". The truth is, this type of lending has helped fund Mulvaney's political career. In the 2015-2016 election cycle, payday lenders like the World

Acceptance Group (which also saw its CFPB charges dropped} Mulvaney, then a congressman from South Carolina, was given $31,700, making him the ninth highest congressional given donations from the industry at the time. Golden Valley, meanwhile, is still functioning and publicising payday loans on its website.

To Mulvaney's credit, he is honest with his donors. Last April, he told an American Bankers Association conference that "We had a hierarchy in my office in Congress. If you're a lobbyist who never gave us any money, I didn't talk to you. If you are a lobbyist who gave us money, I might talk to you." And he certainly has been doing a lot of "talking." The watchdog group Public Citizen contrasted the 30 companies who had the most complaints in the CFPB database to Mulvaney's donors throughout his congressional career. Nineteen of the 30 companies, including eight of the top 10 had donated, via political-action committees, to him.

Mulvaney has stopped enforcement and caused otherwise committed public servants to leave the CFPB in protest. But he hasn't yet to pare back the bureau's statutory authority. Waves of unsuccessful lawsuits against CFPB over the years have helped to initiate legal authority, and Mulvaney hasn't convinced the

Republican-controlled Congress to get rid of his position all together, or to take over the independent agency's budget outright.

That may be because a vast majority of Americans like financial regulation in general and the CFPB in particular. A poll conducted by Americans for Financial Reform found that three-quarters of likely 2018 voters support the existence of the CFPB, and more than half are worried about efforts to limp it .Fortunately, Mick Mulvaney no longer holds this position of shock absorber. I guess public sentiment prevailed.

THE ASIAN FINANCIAL CRISIS

The east Asian countries had remained largely debt-free, evading reliance on International Monetary Fund (IMF) loans or foreign capital except for straight forward investments in manufacturing plants, usually as part of a long-term national goal. But that was before Washington began demanding that the Tiger economies unlock their controlled financial markets to free capital flows, supposedly in the interest of "level playing fields." Like Japan, the East Asian countries went along with the program. The institutional speculators went on the assault, armed with a secret credit line from a group of international banks including Citicorp. They first targeted Thailand, betting that it would be forced to devalue its currency and break from its peg to the dollar. Thailand surrendered, its currency was floated, and it was forced to turn to the IMF for help. The other geese then followed one by one.

Chalmers Johnson wrote in the <u>Los Angeles Times</u> in June 1999:

> The funds easily raped Thailand, Indonesia, and South Korea, then turned the trembling survivors over to the IMF, not to help victims, but to ensure that no Western bank was stuck with a non-performing loan in the devastated countries.

Mark Weisbrot testified before Congress," in this case the IMF not only participated in the financial crisis, it also prescribed policies that that sent the regional economies into a tailspin." The IMF had directed the removal of capital controls, opening the Asian markets to speculation by foreign investors, when what these countries really needed was a supply of foreign exchange reserves to defend themselves against risky currency raids. At a meeting of regional finance ministers in 1997, the government of Japan proposed an Asian Monetary Fund (AMF) that would provide the needed liquidity with fewer stipulations than were imposed by the IMF. But the AMF, which would directly compete with the IMF of the Western bankers, met with vigorous resistance from the U.S. Treasury and failed to materialize. Meanwhile the IMF failed to provide the necessary reserves, while persisting on very high interest rates and "fiscal austerity." The result was a liquidity crisis (a lack of available money) that became a major regional depression.

Weisbrot testified:

> *The human cost of this depression has been staggering.* Years of economic and social progress are being negated, as the unemployed

vie for jobs in sweat shops that they would have previously rejected, and rural poor subsist on leaves, bark, and insects. In Indonesia, the majority of families now have a monthly income less than the amount they would need to buy a subsistence quantity of rice, and nearly 100 million people, half the population, are being pushed below the poverty line.

In 1997, more than 100 billion dollars of Asia's hard currency reserves were relocated in a matter of months into private financial hands. In the wake of currency devaluations, real earnings and employment plummeted practically overnight. The result was mass poverty in countries that had previously been experiencing real economic and social progress. Indonesia was ordered by the IMF to unpeg its currency from the dollar barely three months before the significant plunge of the *rupiah,* its national currency. In an article in <u>Monetary Reform</u> in the winter of 1998-99, Professor Michel Chossudovsky wrote:

> This manipulation of market forces by powerful actors constitutes *a form of financial and economic warfare.* No need to re-colonize lost territory or send in invading armies. In the late twentieth century, the outright "conquest of nations," meaning control over productive assets, labor, and natural resources and institutions, can

be carried out in an impersonal fashion from the corporate boardroom: commands can be dispatched from a computer terminal, or a cell phone. Relevant data are instantly relayed to major financial markets – often resulting in immediate disruptions in the functioning of national economies. "Financial warfare," also applies complex speculative instruments, including the gamut of derivative trade, forward foreign exchange transactions, currency options, hedge funds, index funds, etc. *Speculative instruments have been used with the ultimate purpose of capturing financial wealth and acquiring financial control over productive assets.*

Professor Chossudovsky quoted American billionaire Steve Forbes, who asked rhetorically:

Did the IMF help precipitate the crisis? This agency advocates openness and transparency for national economics, yet it rivals the CIA in cloaking its own operations. Did it, for instance, have secret conversations with Thailand, advocating the devaluation that instantly set off the catastrophic chain of events? …Did IMF prescriptions exacerbate the illness?

These countries monies were knocked down to absurdly low levels.

Chossudovsky warned that the Asian crisis marked the removal of national economic sovereignty and the dismantling of the Bretton Woods institutions safeguarding the strength of national economies. Nations no longer have the ability to control the creation of their own money, which has been usurped by foreign banks.

INTERNATIONAL IMPLICATIONS

The basic plan for the Federal Reserve was drafted at a secret meeting held in November of 1910 at the private resort of J. P. Morgan on Jekyll Island off the coast of Georgia. This culminated in the creation of a bank that was not Federal, but private. The term reserve was used to give Americans a sense of security.

The objective was a cartel. What emerged was a cartel agreement with five objectives: stop the growing competition from the nation's newer banks; obtain a franchise to create money out of nothing for the purpose of lending; get control of the reserves of all banks so that the more reckless ones would not be exposed to currency drains and bank runs; get the taxpayers to pick up the cartel's inevitable losses; and convince Congress that the purpose was to protect the public. It was realized that the bankers would have to become partners with the politicians and the structure of the cartel would have to be a central bank.

Central to understanding these events is that all money in the banking system has been created out of nothing through the process of making loans. The FDIC is not insurance, because the presence of "moral hazard" makes the thing it supposedly protects against more likely to happen. The final cost of the bailout, therefore is passed onto the public in the form of a hidden tax called inflation.

All of the money to accomplish these bailouts was made possible by the Federal Reserve System acting as the "lender of last resort." That was one of the purposes for which it had been created. We must not forget that the phrase "lender of last resort" means that the money is created out of nothing, resulting in the confiscating of our nation's wealth through the hidden tax called inflation.

Our present- day problems within the savings-and - loan industry can be traced back to the Great Depression of the 1930s. Americans were becoming impressed by the theories of socialism and soon embraced the concept that it was proper for government to provide benefits and to protect them from economic hardship.

Once the pattern of government intervention had been established, there began a long, unbroken series of federal rules and regulations that were the source of windfall profits for managers, appraisers, brokers, developers, and builders. They also weakened the industry by encouraging unsound business practices and high-risk investments.

When these ventures failed, and when the value of real estate began to drop, many S&Ls became insolvent. The federal insurance fund was soon depleted, and the government was confronted with its own promise to bail out these companies but not having any money to do so.

The response of regulators was to create accounting gimmicks whereby insolvent thrifts could be made to appear solvent and continue in business. This postponed the inevitable and made matters considerably worse. The failed S&Ls continued to lose billions of dollars each month and added greatly to the ultimate cost of the bailout, all of which would have to be paid by the common man out of taxes and inflation. The ultimate cost is estimated at over one trillion dollars. In the larger view, the S&L industry is a cartel within a cartel. The fiasco could never have happened without the cartel called the Federal Reserve System standing by to create the vast amounts of bailout money pledged by Congress.

The international version of the game called Bailout is similar to the domestic version is that the overall objective is to have the taxpayers cover the defaulted loans so that interest payments can continue going to the banks. The differences are: (1) instead of justifying this as protecting the American public, the pretense that is to save the world from poverty; and (2) the main money pipeline goes from the Federal Reserve through the IMF/World Bank. Otherwise the rules are basically the same.

There is another dimension to the game, however, that involves more than mere profits and scam. It is the conscious and deliberate evolution of the IMF/World Bank into a world central bank with the power to issue a world fiat currency. And that is an important step in an even larger plan to build a true world government within the framework of the United Nations.

47

Economically strong nations are not candidates for surrendering their sovereignty to a world government. Therefore, through "loans" that will never be paid back, the IMF/World Bank directs the massive transfer of wealth from the industrialized nations to the less developed nations. This ongoing process eventually drains their economies to the point where they also will be in need of assistance. No longer capable of independent action, they will accept the loss of sovereignty in return for international aid. less developed countries, on the other hand, are being brought into the New World Order along an entirely different route. Many of these countries are ruled by petty tyrants who care little for their people except how to extract more taxes from them without causing a revolt. Loans from the IMF/World Bank are used primarily to perpetuate themselves and their ruling parties in power---and that is exactly what the IMF/World Bank intends. Rhetoric about helping the poor notwithstanding, the true goal of the transfer of wealth disguised as loans is to get control over the leaders of the less developed countries. After these despots get used to the taste of such an unlimited supply of sweet cash, they will never be able to break the habit. They will be content---already are content----to become little gold-plated cogs in the giant machinery of world government. Ideology means nothing to them: capitalist, communist, socialist, fascist, what does it matter so long as the money keeps coming. The IMF/World Bank literally is *buying* these countries and using our money to do it.

Precious metals were the first commodity money to appear in history and ever since have been proven by actual experience to be the only reliable base for an honest monetary system. Gold, as the basis of money, can take several forms: bullion, coins, and fully backed paper receipts. Man has been plagued throughout history with the false theory that the quantity of money is important, specifically that more money is better than less. This has led to perpetual manipulation and expansion of the money supply. During one period when the Bank of England forced the colonies to abandon their fiat money, general prosperity quickly returned. The supply through such practices as coin clipping, debasement of the coin content, and, in latter centuries, the issuance of more paper receipts than there was gold to back them. In every case, these practices have led to economic and political disaster. In these rare instances where man has refrained from manipulating the money supply and has allowed it to be determined by free-market production of the gold supply, the result has been prosperity and tranquility.

Fiat money is paper money without precious metal backing which people by law are required to accept. During one period when the Bank of England forced the colonies to abandon their fiat money, general prosperity quickly returned. Fractional money always degenerates into pure fiat money.

When money is created out of nothing, the true interest rate is not 8% or 9% or even 22%. It is infinity. It is easier than printing and, because the process is not understood by the public, it is politically safe. Who cares if the scheme is destructive? Here is the perfect tool for obtaining unlimited funding for politicians and endless profits for bankers. And best of all, the little people who pay the bills for both groups have no idea what is being done to them. They began lending out pieces of paper that said they were receipts, but which in fact were *counterfeit*. The public could not tell one from the other and accepted both of them as money. From that point forward, the receipts in circulation exceeded the gold held in reserve, and the age of fractional-reserve banking had dawned. This led immediately to what would become an almost unbroken record to then to the present: a record of inflation, booms and busts, suspension of payments, bank failures, repudiation of currencies, and recurring spasms of economic chaos.

The Bank of England was formed in 1694 by the Rothschilds to institutionalize fractional-reserve banking. As the world's first central bank, it introduced the concept of a partnership between bankers and politicians. The politicians would receive spendable money (created out of nothing by the bankers) without having to raise taxes. In return, the bankers would receive a commission on the transaction---deceptively called interest---which would continue in perpetuity.

The American dollar has no intrinsic value. It is the classic example of fiat money with no limit to the quantity that can be produced. Its primary value lies in the willingness of people to accept it and, to that end, legal tender laws require them to do so. It is true that our money is created out of nothing, but it is more accurate to say that it is based on debt. In one sense, therefore, our money is created out of less than nothing. The entire money system would vanish into bank vaults and computer chips if all debts were repaid. Under the present System, therefore, our leaders cannot allow a serious reduction in either the consumer or national debt. Charging interest on pretended loans is usury, and that has become institutionalized under the Federal Reserve System. The Slight-of Hand Mechanism by which the Feds converts debt into money may seem complicated at first, but it is simple if one remembers that the process is not intended to be logical but confuse and deceive. The end product of the Slight-of-Hand Mechanism is artificial expansion of the money supply, which is the root cause of the hidden tax called inflation. This expansion then leads to contraction and, together, they produce the destructive boom-bust cycle that has plagued mankind throughout history wherever fiat money has existed.

Wars great and small, have always been a plague to Europe, but it was not until they were easy to finance through central banking and fiat money that they became virtually perpetual. For example, the following war chronicle begins immediately following the formation of the Bank of England which, as you recall, was created for the specific purpose of financing a war:

1689—1697 The War of the League of Augsburg

1702—1713 The War of Spanish Succession

1739—1742 The War of Jenkin's Ear

1744—1748 The War of Austrian Succession

1754—1763 The French and Indian War

1793—1801 The War against Revolutionary France

1803—1815 The Napoleonic Wars

The fact that different branches of the Rothschild network might also be providing funds for the enemy was pragmatically ignored. Thus, a time- honored practice among financiers was born: profiting from both sides.

A study of these and similar events reveals a personality profile, not just of the Rothschilds, but that special breed of international financiers whose success is typically built upon certain character traits. Those include cold objectivity, immunity to patriotism, and indifference to human condition.

As long as the mechanism of central banking exist, it will be to such men an irresistible temptation to convert debt into perpetual war and war into perpetual debt.

To finance the early stages of World War 1, England and France had borrowed heavily from investors in America and had selected the House of Morgan as sales agent for their bonds. Many Americans thought Morgan was the richest man in the world only to realize later that he was just a captain under the Rothschilds.   Morgan also acted as their U. S purchasing agent for war materials, thus profiting from both ends of the cash flow: once when the money was borrowed and again when it was spent.

The only way to save the British Empire, to restore the value of the bonds, and to sustain the Morgan cash flow was for the United States government to provide the money. But since neutral nations were prohibited from doing that by treaty, America would have to be brought into the war.

Morgan had created an international shipping cartel, including Germany's merchant fleet, which maintained a near monopoly on the high seas. Only the British Cunard Lines remained aloof. The Lusitania was owned by Cunard and operated in competition with Morgan's cartel. The Lusitania was built to military specifications and was registered with British Admiralty as an armed auxiliary cruiser. She carried passengers as a cover to conceal her real mission, which was to bring contraband war materials from the United States.

The British knew that to draw the United States into the war would mean the difference between defeat and victory, and anything that would accomplish that was proper--

-even the coldly calculated sacrifice of one of her great ships with Englishmen aboard. But the trick was to have Americans on board also to create the proper emotional climate in the United States. As the Lusitania moved into hostile waters where the German U-boat was known to be operating, First Lord of the Admiralty, Winston Churchill, ordered her destroyer protection to abandon her. This, plus the fact that she had been ordered to travel at reduced speed, made her an easy target.

The deed had been done, and it set into motion great waves of revulsion against the Germans. These waves eventually flooded through Washington and swept the United States into war. Within days of the declaration, Congress voted $1 billion in credit for England and France. $200 million was sent to England immediately and was applied to the Morgan account. The vast quantity of money needed to finance the war was created by the Federal Reserve System, which means it was collected from Americans through that hidden tax called inflation. Within just five years, this tax had taken fully one-half of all they had saved. The infinitely high cost in American blood was added to the bill.

Headquartered in England, the Rhodes inner-most directorate was called the Round Table. In other countries, there were established subordinate structures called Round table Groups. The Round Table Group in the United States became known as the Council on Foreign Relations. The

CFR, which was initially dominated by J. P. Morgan and later by the Rockefellers, is the most powerful group in America today. It is even more powerful than the federal government, because almost all of the key positions in government are held by its members. In other words, it is the United States government.

The American contingent in Russia disguised itself as a Red Cross mission allegedly doing humanitarian work. Cashing in on their close friendship with Trotsky and Lenin, they obtained profitable business concessions from the new government which returned their initial investment many times over.

The Red Cross Mission of New York financiers threw support to the Bolsheviks and, in return, received economic rewards in the form of rights to Russia's natural resources plus contracts for construction and supplies. The continued participation in the economic development of Russia and Eastern Europe since that time indicates that this relationship has survived to the present day. These financiers are not pro-communist. Their motivation is profit and power. They are now working to bring Russia and the United States into a world government which they expect to control. War and threats of war are tools to prod the masses toward the acceptance of that goal. It is essential, therefore, that the United States and the industrialized nations of the world have credible enemies. As these words are being written, Russia is wearing the mask of peace and cooperation. But we have seen that before. We may yet see the return of the Evil Empire when the timing is right. U. S. government and megabank funding, first of Russia, and now of Chinese and Middle-East military capabilities, cannot be understood without this insight.

The Constitution prohibits both the states and the federal government from issuing fiat money. This was the deliberant intent of the Founding Fathers who had bitter experience with fiat money before and especially during the Revolutionary War. In response to the need to have a precisely defined monetary unit Congress adopted the Spanish dollar then currently in use and defined the content of that dollar to be 371.25 grains of pure silver. With the establishment of a federal mint, American silver dollars were issued in accordance with that standard, and gold Eagles also were produced which were equal in value to ten silver dollars. Most importantly, free coinage was established wherein Americans were able to convert their raw silver and gold into national coins officially certified by the government as to their intrinsic value. The product of these measures was a period of sound money and great economic prosperity, a period that would come to an end only when the next generation of Americans forgot to read their history and returned to the use of paper money and "bills of credit." The issuance of bank notes had been severely limited, but that was largely offset by the increasing use of checkbook money, which had no limits at all on its issue.

None dealt with the real problem, which was fractional reserve banking itself. They concentrated on proposals on how to make it work. All of these proposals were tried and they failed.

The economic chaos and conflict of this period was the major cause of the Civil War. Lincoln made it clear during his public speeches that slavery was not the issue. The basic problem was that the North and South were dependent on each other for trade. The industrialized North sold its products to the South which sold its cotton to the North. The south also had a similar trade with Europe, and that was an annoyance to the North. Europe was selling many products at lower prices, and the North was losing market share. Northern politicians passed protectionist legislation putting import duties on industrialized products. This all but stopped the importation of European goods and forced the South to buy from the North at higher prices. Europe retaliated by curtailing the purchase of American cotton. That hurt the South even more. It was a classic case of legalized plunder, and the South wanted out.

Meanwhile there were powerful forces in Europe who wanted to see America led in civil war. If she could be split into two hostile countries, there would be less obstacle to European expansion on the North American continent. France was eager to capture Mexico and graft it onto a new empire which would include many of the Southern states as well.

57

England, on the other hand, had military forces poised along the Canadian border ready for action. Political agitators funded and organized from Europe, were active on both sides of the Mason-Dixon line. America had become a target in a ruthless game of world economics and politics.

America's bloodiest and most devastating war was fought because of clashing economic interests, facilitated by slave labor. At the heart of this conflict were questions of legalized plunder, banking monopolies, and even European expansion into Latin America.

A national banking system was created to convert government bonds into fiat money and the people lost over half of their monetary assets to the hidden tax of inflation.

GLOBAL CREDIT

A large chunk of consumer spending is on the purchase of homes and obtaining mortgages. Housing in turn fuels appliance sales, home furnishings and construction. In 1940 44% of U. S. citizens owned their own homes. By 1960 62% of Americans owned their homes and by 1980, they own 70% of all housing.

A couple of days after the 9/11 bombing of the World Trade Center shock, government officials were urging citizens, above all, to shop and work is ample testimony to the significance of consumption in the effective working of our economy and indeed the whole society.

The Sub-prime mortgage market differs from the prime (primary) market as it comprises all those people who do not meet the criteria for a mortgage in the mainstream market. The adoption of the Depository Institutions Deregulatory and Monetary Control Act in 1980 was part of the deregulation drive that eliminated many of the restrictions to lending. This resulted in loans reaching unprecedented levels which led to the mainstream market becoming saturated and reaching its peak of profitability. Those with dubious credit histories and of low income were turned away from mainstream mortgages at a time when the market was buoyant due to consumer spending and borrowing.

Global Gross Domestic Product
(GDP) 2007

1.	US	13.8t
2.	Japan	4.3t
3.	Germany	3.3t
4.	China	3.2t
5.	UK	2.7t
6.	France	2.5t
7.	Italy	2.1t
8.	Spain	1.4t
9.	Canada	1.4t
10.	Brazil	1.3t

- T=trillion

	National Debt
1.US	12.8t
2.UK	11.5t
3.Germany	4.4t
4.France	4.3t
5.Italy	2.3t
6.Netherlands	2.2t
7.Spain	2.0t
8.Ireland	1.8t
9.Japan	1.4t

The Sub-prime market was carved out after this point as 25% of the US population fell into this category and represented a market opportunity. US lenders gave mortgages to people who had little means to pay for a mortgage and charged them a rate of interest much higher than the commercial due to the increased default risk. They issued these mortgages safe in the knowledge that if the buyer defaults, they would be able to repossess the property, and resell it in a buoyant property market. By the start of 2007, the sub-prime market was valued at more than $1.3 trillion.

Traditional banks stayed away from this risky market and instead remained focused on prime lending and questioned some of the business practices of sub-prime companies such as their aggressive lending and accounting practices. Between 1994 and 1997 the number of sub-prime lenders tripled, going from 70 to 210. Because such institutions were not banks, they possessed no customer deposits and in order to expand many lenders turned to the stock market for funding. Companies such as Money Store AMRESCO Inc, Dallas and Ames Financial Corporation, all raised capital through placing some of their companies on the stock market. Relatively young lenders such as Long Beach Financial Corporation; Irvine, California- based New Century Financial Corporation; Delta Funding Corporation;

and Cityscape Financial all took their companies 100% public. By the end of 1997, the top 10 lenders accounted for 38% of all sub-prime lending.

The collapse of the Russian ruble and long-term capital management in 1997 resulted in a number of foreclosures leading to the demise of six of the top 10 sub-prime lenders. This left an enormous vacuum in the sub-prime industry that resulted in a series of acquisitions by commercial banks such as Washington Mutual's acquisition of Long Beach Financial Corporation. Associates First Capital, the third -largest sub -prime originator at the time, was purchased by Citigroup Inc. In 2001, Chase Manhattan Mortgage Corporation acquired Advanta Mortgage Corporation, the 16th -largest sub-prime lender at the time for $1 billion. In 2003, HSBC Finance Corporation acquired sub-prime powerhouse Household Finance, which had earned the rank of the largest sub-prime lender in the two years prior to its acquisition by HSBC. Mortgage brokers did not lend their own money. There was no correlation between loan performance and compensation. There were big financial incentives for selling complex, adjustable rate mortgages for such companies since this would earn higher commissions. In 2004 Mortgage brokers originated 68% of all residential loans, with sub-prime loans accounting for 43% of brokerage's total loans.

Most sub-prime lenders then invented another way of making money in a sector which was already highly risky. Many lenders wanted to insure they didn't lose out at possible money- making opportunities in the sub-prime market and developed a number of sub-prime products. This was achieved by breaking down the value of the sub-prime market and various home loans into financial sausage meat -just as wholesome as the real-world equivalent and selling them on to other institutions. Debt was sold to a third party, who would then receive the loan repayments and pay fee for the privilege. Thus, debt became tradeable just like a car. The ability to securitize provided a way for risk to be sliced and diced and spread, thereby allowing more mortgages to be sold. Since 1994 the securitization rate of sub-prime loans increased from 32% to over 77% of total sub-prime loans. This process effectively increased the number of financial institutions with a stake in the sub-prime mortgage market. This was allowed to happen due to the manner in which the original sub-prime loans were scrutinized.

Many institutions including Wall Street investment banks became owners of collateral debt obligations (CDO's). These are bonds created by a process of deconstructing and re-engineering asset-backed securities. This essentially works by providing investors with access to regular payments received from debt payers in return for paying to have access to the CDO as well as management fees. Wall Street investment banks made investments in the cash flows of the assets, rather than a direct investment in the underlying asset.

Many institutions also became owners of mortgage-backed securities (MBS) which were created out of the repackaging of sub-prime loans. In simple terms, this is where a bank sells asset of debts as one product. In return for a fee the new holder of this debt obligation received the regular loan repayments. In most cases such a debt forms part of a pool of mortgage debts lumped together into a form of asset or bond, each with different degrees of risk attached to them. The owners of MBS's actually do not know the source of where the payments are coming from or even which sectors, they are being exposed to. At that time the MBS market was worth $6 trillion, even more than U.S. treasury bonds. The difference between CDO's and MBS's is in the latter the property is placed as collateral.

In any event of a downturn in the housing market it would not only be the sub-prime providers who would lose out, but now all those who purchased collateral products would be exposed.

U.S. home loans had been pooled and packaged into tradeable securities by Wall Street banks before being put onto financial institutions around the world. As they were bought and sold, these mortgage-backed securities were valued according to ratings given to them by the credit rating agencies. Credit agencies (dominated by the big three; Moody's, Standard & Poor's and Fitch) classify the risk of these repackaged securities according to their exposure to risky markets. CDO's were classified into tranches, the highest tranche was perceived to be very low risk and was often given a AAA rating – the same rating as high-grade US Treasury Bonds. This is because in the event of default the first to incur the loss would be the lower tranches and not the top tier. The mathematical models and simulations that the banks relied upon did predict a scenario where defaults would become so numerous that even the top tier AAA-rated tranches would be affected.

As the housing sector continued to inflate, due to the appetite for housing by Americans, the sub-prime sector continued to grow. Commercial banks entered what they considered a buoyant market that could only rise, many Americans refinanced their homes by taking out second mortgages against the added value to use funds for consumer spending. The first sign that the US housing bubble was in trouble was on the 2nd of April 2007 when New Century Inc. the largest sub -prime mortgage lender in the US declared bankruptcy due to the increasing number of defaults from borrowers. In the previous month 25 sub-prime lenders declared bankruptcy, announcing significant losses, with some putting themselves up for sale. This was in hindsight the beginning of the end.

The crisis then spread to the owners of collateralized debt who were now in the position where the payments they were promised from the debts they had purchased was being defaulted upon. By being owners of various complex products, the constituent elements of such products resulted in many holders of such debt to sell other investments in order to balance losses incurred from exposure to the sub-prime sector or what is known as 'covering a position'. This second round of selling to shore up funds and meet brokerage margin requirements is what caused the collapse in share prices around the world in August 2007, with the market getting into a vicious circle of falling prices leading to the further sales of shares to shore up losses. This type of behavior is typical of a Capitalistic market crash and is what caused world-wide share values to plummet. What made matters worse were that many investors caught in this vicious spiral of declining prices did not just sell sub-prime and related products; they sold anything that could be sold. This is why share prices plummeted across the world and not just in those directly related sub-prime mortgages.

International institutes who poured their money into the US housing sector realized that they will not actually receive their money that they loaned out to investors as individual sub-prime were defaulting in mass on such loans. This resulted in all those who took positions in the housing sector not being able to pay the institutes they borrowed money from. It was for this reason central banks across the world intervened in the global economy in an unprecedented manner providing large amounts of cash to ensure that such banks and institutes did not go bankrupt. The European Central Bank, America's Federal Reserve and the Japanese and Australian central banks injected over $300 billion into the banking system within 48 hours in a bid to avert a financial crisis. They stepped in when banks, such as Sentinel, a large American investment house, stopped investors from withdrawing their money, spooked by sudden and unexpected losses from bad loans in the

American mortgage market, other institutions followed suit and suspended normal lending. Intervention by the world's central banks in order to avert crisis cost them over $800 billion after only seven days.

Banks across the world fund the majority of their lending by borrowing from other banks or by raising money through the financial markets. The borrowing between banks is undertaken on a daily basis in order to balance their books. The realization dawned that sub-prime mortgage backed securities existed across the banking sector in the portfolios of banks and hedge funds around the world, from DNP Paribus to Bank of China, many lenders stopped offering loans. Some only offered loans at very high interest rates and most banks stopped lending to other banks to shore up their books. As no bank knew how much each bank was exposed to the sub-prime crisis many refused to lend to other bank. This led to a credit crunch whereby those banks who made the majority of their loans from borrowed money found credit was drying up.

The first indication that the housing crisis was not going to affect the US and spread to the wider global economy was the effective collapse of Britain's Northern Rock. Northern Rock was the 5th largest mortgage lender in the UK and funded its lending by borrowing 80%

from the financial markets. As the credit markets froze, they requested the Bank of England, as the lender of last resort in the UK, for a liquidity support facility due to problems in raising funds in the money markets. This created a run on the bank as depositors withdrew their money in panic. The British Government took the controversial decision to nationalize Northern Rock as its collapse would have inevitably spread to other banks as panic-stricken depositors attempted to withdraw their savings – the whole banking sector would have collapsed.

A similar scenario occurred in March 2008 with Bear Stearns one of the world's largest investment banks as it was forced to write off three of its investment funds in the sub-prime market. Bear Stearns problems escalated when rumors spread about its liquidity crisis which in turn eroded investor confidence in the firm.

With the housing sector the driving engine for the US economy for the last decade, its collapse would have severe repercussions across the global economy as much of the world banks placed their money through complex securitization in the sub-prime market. With the US economy considered already in recession this will have world-wide affects as the US economy drives the world economy due to its huge consumption.

Major Sub-Prime Losses
(As of June2008)

Citigroup:	$40.7bn
UBS:	$38bn
Merrill Lynch:	$31.7bn
HSBC:	$15.6bn
Bank of America:	$14.9bn
Morgan Stanley:	$12.6bn
Royal Bank of Scotland:	$12bn
J.P. Morgan Chase:	$9.7bn
Washington Mutual:	$8.3bn
Deutsche Bank:	$7.5bn
Wachovia:	$ 7.3bn
Credit Agricole:	$6.6bn
Credit Suisse	$6.3bn
Mizuho Financial	$5.5bn
Bear Sterns:	$3.2bn
Barclays:	$3.2bn

MALASIA vs. WORLD BANK

Most of the Asian geese succumbed to the floating currency trick, but Malaysia stood its ground. Malaysia Prime Minister Mahathir Mohammad said the IMF was using the financial crisis to enable giant international corporations to take over Third World economies. He contended:

> They see our troubles as a means to accept certain regimes, to open our markets to foreign companies to do business without any conditions. [The IMF] says it will give you money if you open up your economy, but doing so will cause all our banks, companies and industries to belong to foreigners.

> They call for reform but this may result in millions thrown out of work. I told the top official of the IMF that if companies were to close, workers would be retrenched, but he said this didn't matter as bad companies must be closed. I told him that companies became bad because of external factors, so

you can't bankrupt them as it was not their fault. But the IMF wants the companies to go bankrupt.

Mahathir was emphatic that his government had not failed. Rather, it had been victimized along with the rest of the region by the international system. He blamed the collapse of Asia's currency on an organized attack by giant international hedge funds. Because they profited from relatively small differences in asset values, the speculators were prepared to create sudden, massive and uncontrollable outflows of capital that would wreck national economies by causing capital flight. He charged, "This deliberate devaluation of a currency of a country by currency traders purely for profit is a serious infringement of the rights of independent nations." Mahathir said he had appealed to the international agencies to regulate international trading to no avail, so he had been forced to take matters into his own hands. He had imposed capital and exchange controls, a policy aimed at shifting the focus from catering to foreign capital to motivate national development. He fixed the exchange rate of the *ringgit* (the Malaysian national currency) and ordered that it be traded only in Malaysia. These statutes did not affect genuine investors, he said, who could bring in foreign funds, convert them into ringgit for local investment, and apply to the Central Bank to convert their ringgit back into foreign currency as needed.

Western economists waited for the economic disaster they presumed would follow; but capital controls actually helped to stabilize the system. Before controls were imposed, Malaysia's economy had contracted by 7.5 percent. The year afterwards, growth projections went as high as 5 percent. Joseph Stiglitz, chief economist for the World Bank, acknowledged in 1999 that the Bank had been "humbled" by Malaysia's performance. It was a tacit admission that *the World Banks's position had been wrong*.

ISLAMIC POSITION ON USURY (RIBAH)

A *riba*-based economic system assumes a total divorce between the Devine will and human life, resulting in the assumption that man is the absolute master of his world, uncommitted by any responsibility towards God or an obligation to respect his teachings or commands. It also suggests that man is free as to how he accumulates, enjoys and uses his wealth, and that in this regard he has no obligation whatsoever towards God or any liability to humanity. This is a clear overreach of man's limited free will.

Of course, man-made laws may on occasion intervene to restrict this freedom by setting the rates of *riba* or banning certain fraudulent and illegal practices, but this is usually prompted by expediency and popular

74

convention rather than beliefs in the principle laid down by a higher Devine authority. For example, a real estate brokers publication with a usury ceiling listed on the cover.

A *riba* based system is based on the erroneous concept that the accumulation and enjoyment of wealth, regardless of the means, is the ultimate objective of human life, which explains the resulting reckless and viciousness for money-making. American Telephone and Telegraph is the world's largest distributer of pornographic videos to hotels and motels.

These influential individuals and institutions not only control the world economy and international wealth, but they also have enormous influence in several other walks of life with the aim of embellishing their role and position in the world. Since they are unscrupulous and unprincipled and look with distain on religion and morality, it is to their advantage to subvert religious belief and promote moral degradation, promiscuity, and excessive spending. They orchestrate the world economy for their own benefit, manufacturing and fueling regular economic crisis in various parts of the world and distracting economic and industrial production away from the common world interest to areas that will give them the greatest benefit and control of international wealth.

The majority of the capital today is under the real control of a few thousand people. Landlords, industrialists, farmers and traders who borrow from the banks, as well as workers and ordinary consumers, are no more than laborers working for the benefit of those in possession and control of capital.

Moneylenders try to make maximum gains by lending their money, and therefore favor a squeeze on the money supply to cause a rise in the cost of borrowing. This eventually leads to a slowdown in the economy and a rise in unemployment, and inflation. This fall in demand forces the moneylenders to reduce the cost of borrowing, and a new cycle of growth and prosperity begins, only to lead to another recession and more misery for borrowers and consumers. It is this vicious cycle of boom and bust that brings about the regular international economic crisis.

Moral and practical considerations are inextricably linked. In all his actions, man is governed by the terms of God's covenant, he is here with a mission and a responsibility and will have to account for his actions in the Hereafter.

Currently, it has opened the gates for some of the most sinister and corrupting forms of investment ever known, such as the pornography, drug trade, prostitution, all in the hunt of guaranteed astronomical profits. Borrowed money is not used in the service of humanity but for maximizing profit, regardless of the nature of the trade or the method by which that profit is realized.

Islam is a comprehensive way of life. Its economic system completely eliminates the need for *riba and* organizes the social life of the community in such a way as to remove *riba* altogether. At the same time, it maintains the balance and progress of economic, social and human development in the society.

Under Islam there is no need for the invalidation and removal of existing economic and financial institutions, such as banks and commercial companies, which play an essential role in modern economic development. Islam can change these institutions and enable them to perform along the sound and constructive rules and regulations that it lays down.

Muslims are commanded to invest their money and seek the growth and development of their wealth, by scrupulous and legitimate means, without taking advantage of others or encroaching on their rights. Besides, it is not allowed to try to pervert, in any way, the fair circulation of capital and wealth in the society. The Qur'an states that wealth "should not be the monopoly of the rich among you" (al-Hashr 59:7).

Muslims have to accept that it is a conceptual impossibility that God Almighty should prohibit something that is essential for the perpetuation and preservation of human life. By the same token, no practice that is inherently corrupt could ever be vital for the organization and progress of human life. A Muslim who truly believes in God as the creator, preserver and controller of life and the world cannot conceive that God would forbid anything that is vital, or prescribe anything that is vile or obscene. The implication that the economic and financial institutions cannot survive or function without *riba* is simply a myth and a lie maintained by big business and international vested interests. *Riba*-free economies have existed and performed very successfully. To revive them today requires determination and a collective, well considered international effort by at least the Muslim countries of the world, in order to restore some hope of future stability, prosperity, and real peace and justice in our world.

الَّذِينَ يَأْكُلُونَ الرِّبَا لَا يَقُومُونَ إِلَّا كَمَا يَقُومُ الَّذِي يَتَخَبَّطُهُ الشَّيْطَانُ مِنَ الْمَسِّ ذَٰلِكَ بِأَنَّهُمْ قَالُوا إِنَّمَا الْبَيْعُ مِثْلُ الرِّبَا وَأَحَلَّ اللَّهُ الْبَيْعَ وَحَرَّمَ الرِّبَا فَمَن جَاءَهُ مَوْعِظَةٌ مِّن رَّبِّهِ فَانتَهَىٰ فَلَهُ مَا سَلَفَ وَأَمْرُهُ إِلَى اللَّهِ وَمَنْ عَادَ فَأُولَٰئِكَ أَصْحَابُ النَّارِ هُمْ فِيهَا خَالِدُونَ ﴿٢٧٥﴾ يَمْحَقُ اللَّهُ الرِّبَا وَيُرْبِي الصَّدَقَاتِ وَاللَّهُ لَا يُحِبُّ كُلَّ كَفَّارٍ أَثِيمٍ ﴿٢٧٦﴾

Those who gorge themselves on usury cannot rise up except as he may rise up whom Satan has confounded with his touch. That is because they say, "Trade is just the same as usury." But God has made trade lawful and usury

forbidden. He who receives an admonition from his Lord, and there upon desists (from usury) may retain his past gains, and God shall be his ultimate judge. Those who revert to the practice (of usury) are indeed the inmates of the Fire, wherein they shall abide. God blots out usury and makes charitable offerings grow and increase. God does not love confirmed disbelievers who persist in wrongdoing.
Qur'an (al Bakarah)2:275-276

It is a terrifying image, far more effective than any threat or admonition. The image of a person possessed by the devil is an evocative and terrifying one, most effective in preventing usurers and in conveying the message to others. It arouses the human conscience and brings home the horrible reality of the effects of usury on the individuals as well as society as a whole.

Most commentators have suggested that the *surah* refers to rising before God on the Day of Judgement. This is a metaphor for what actually occurs in life on this earth. This interpretation is supported by a later passage warning usurers of an impending war against them by God and His Messenger, which we can see going on in the world today. The whole world is struggling under the dire consequence of a pervasive international *riba*-based financial system.

Abu Sa'id al-Khudri reports that the Prophet said: "Gold for gold, silver for silver, wheat for wheat, barley for barley, dates for dates and salt for salt, (these should be exchanged) measure for measure, from hand to hand (on the spot). If either party takes or gives anything more, both are guilty of usury" (Bukhari and Muslim).

Al-Khudri also reports that when Bilal, the Abyssinian Companion of the Prophet, once brought the Prophet some dates of excellent quality, the Prophet immediately asked where he had obtained them. Bilal said he had traded for some dates of lower quality that were in his possession, two measures for one. The Prophet was extremely annoyed and said: "This is *riba* itself! It is the very thing! Do not ever do it. If you wish to buy good dates, sell your dates for something else and then buy the good ones with what you receive." (Bukhari and Muslim)

That *riba al-nasi'ah* is usurious is self-explanatory. It includes an increased payment and time enlargement, the two essential elements of usurious conduct. In riba al-fadl there have to be real differences in quality of the same commodity which give rise to an increase of one over the other. This is clear in Bilal's transaction, condemned as usurious, since it assigned two different values to the two types of dates. The Prophet ordered that one type of dates should be sold for cash, which is then used by the seller to purchase the other type, removing all suspicion of usury.

The requirement of traded goods simultaneously, "hand to hand "is important to avoid any difference in the two quantities due to a lapse in time which could affect their respective values. It also signifies how sensitive the Prophet was to any hint of usury, and how determined was his approach in uprooting it.

"Those who gorge themselves on usury cannot rise up as he may rise up whom Satan has confounded with his touch." This is a reference not only to those who charge *riba*, but also to society as a whole.

Jabir ibn 'Abdullah reports that the Prophet has cursed the person who charges *riba*, as well as the one who pays it, and those who witness it and the one who writes the contract, saying: "They bear similar responsibility" (Muslim, Ahmad, Abu Daw'ud and Tirmidhi).

It is a fact that no fair- minded person cannot refute. The majority of people in the most affluent and materially advanced countries, such as the United States of America and Sweden, lead the most miserable lives. Anxiety, depression and boredom are devouring people's lives who, despite their affluence and energy, are propelled to a culture of fads and mental and sexual perversions, and all kinds of anti-social escapist behavior that permits them no peace or security.

The fundamental cause of this prevalence is the spiritual wilderness in which Western societies are living today. For, in spite of the prosperity and material wellbeing they enjoy, these societies lack the spiritual reassurance and faith that can only come with the belief in God. They have separated themselves from their own souls and no longer have any universal goals or aims to aspire to. They have lost faith in human life and man's mission and role in the world as defined in God's covenant with mankind.

Those with vested interest objected to the condemnation and the abolition of *riba*, claiming that *"Trade is just the same as usury." But God has made trade lawful and usury forbidden.*" Their debate rested on the false supposition that the objective of both trading and *riba* was to make gains and benefits, but trading is open to the risk of profit and loss and requires real tangible input from the trader, while *riba* transactions are aimed at bringing guaranteed gains for the lender in any case. That is the crucial difference between the two. Any transactions involving a guaranteed for the lender, under all circumstances, are usurious and forbidden. There can be no argument on this point. God has permitted trading for many reasons that make it beneficial for human life, and the absence of guaranteed returns is first among them.

However, Islam faced the situation existing at the time with realism, preventing any kind of economic and social upheaval. It stated its new rules effective immediately and turned a new page with respect to what was going on previously. The surah says: *"He who receives an admonition from his Lord, and thereupon desists (from usury) may retain his past gains, and God shall be his ultimate judge."* It seems to suggest exoneration for previous usurious activities would be left to God's grace, thereby providing individuals with a stronger incentive to cease and conduct their trade without *riba*. Nevertheless, it goes on to alert those who go back to such practices that they *"are indeed the inmates of the Fire, where in they shall abide."* It declares with power and authority for the benefit of those who might delude themselves that the Hereafter was a long way away, that, *"God blots out usury and makes charitable offerings grow and increase. God does not love confirmed disbelievers who persist in wrongdoing.*"

God's words have come true. There is no evidence that no society has built its economy on usury and seen real prosperity, peace, security or happiness. A society may indeed be outwardly wealthy, fruitful and affluent, but these are not necessarily the signs of a blessed and fortunate society. Social welfare, integrity and cohesion are only found in societies constructed on charity, tolerance, compassion and open-handedness, and in which they compete only for the pleasure and grace of God Almighty.

"God does not love confirmed disbelievers who persist in wrongdoing."

This statement clearly signifies that those who persist with *riba,* after all that has been said about it, are guilty of grave wrongdoing and condemned by God. Evidently those who legalize what God has forbidden are guilty and damned, even if they assert their belief in Islam with all the power at their disposal.

The Arabic word riba' literally means "increase in" or "addition to "to anything. Technically it was

85

applied to that additional sum which the creditor charged from debtor at fixed rate on the principle he lent, that is, interest. At the time of the revelations of the Quran, interest was extracted in several ways. For instance, a person sold something and fixed a time limit for payment of its price, and if the buyer failed to pay it within a fixed period, he was allowed more time but had to pay an additional sum. Or a person lent a sum of money and was asked by the debtor to pay it back together with an agreed additional sum of money within a fixed period.

The Quran compares the money lender to a mad man. Just as the madman loses his sense on account of his disordered intellect, in the same way the money-lender is so mad for money-making that he separates himself from common sense. He is so senseless foolish and impudent that he does not mind how his selfishness and greed are cutting at the very root of human brotherhood and tearing down the common good of mankind. He doesn't care a bit that that he is acquiring prosperity at the expense of many.

They based their rational on a wrong theory and did not see the fundamental difference between profit and interest. Their proof was that if profit on capitol was lawful in trade, why should interest invested in loans be unlawful? And the Arab money-lenders were not alone in debating like this. The person, who lends a sum of money to another, could himself make profit from it and that the debtor actually invested it in a profitable business. Why should not the creditor, then get a portion of the profit for his productive credit? However, what they forget is that *there is no business in the whole world where there is fixed and guaranteed profit without the risk.* In trade, commerce, industry, agriculture, etc. one has to spend both labor and capital and the same time one has to face probable loss, without any guaranteed fixed profit. For the present, let us put aside the case of the debtor who borrows money for *consumption* and not for *production*, and also the issue of the rate of interest. Let us compare the case of the money-lender who lends money at a moderate rate of interest for profitable rate of business with the case of those engaged in other kinds of business. They dedicate their whole time, labor, talent and invest their own capital, etc. and work day and night so that the business may become profitable by virtue of their own attempts. But even then, they are not guaranteed any guaranteed fixed profit, and have to bear all the risk. On the contrary, the money-lender, who lends his capital only, goes on experiencing a fixed amount of profit, without any risk whatsoever. By what reasoning and on what principles of logic, justice and economics is it right for him to receive a fixed amount of profit?

The fundamental difference between profit and interest that produces different moral and economic results is this:

1. The settlement of profit between the buyer and the seller is made on equal terms. The buyer purchases the property he needs and the seller gets the profit for the time, labor and brains he employs in providing the article to the buyer. In contrast to this, in the case of interest, obviously the debtor cannot settle the transaction on equal terms with the creditor because of his weaker position. As far as the money-lender is concerned, he gets that fixed sum of interest which he considers as his profit. If the debtor spends the borrowed money in fulfilling his personal needs, the *time factor does not bring any profit at all*. And if he invested the money in trade, commerce, industry, agriculture etc., then there are equal chances of profit or loss. Therefore, lending money on interest might bring a guaranteed and fixed profit to one and an uncertain and indefinite profit to the other.

2. The trader charges his profit, however high it might be, once for all but the money-lender goes on charging interest over and over again and it goes on increasing with the passage of time. The profit which the debtor makes on the money of the creditor, however large it may be, has after all its own limits, but there is no limit to interest the creditor may charge on his money. He may, as sometimes actually happens, receive all the earnings of the debtor, which may even deprive him of all the means of livelihood or the articles of personal use and still might have the same amount against him that was at the time of borrowing.

3. The transaction in trade comes to an end as soon as the article and its price change hands. After this the buyer is not required to return anything to the seller. As regards the rent of furniture, house, land, etc., the lent thing is not itself spent up but is returned to the owner after the term. But in the case of the principle the debtor has to spend it first and then to reproduce it and return it, to the creditor along with its interest. The debtor runs a double risk, he has to reproduce the *principle* and the *interest*.

From the above it becomes quite clear that even from the economic point of view, trade helps construct society but interest guides to its ruin. As for the moral point of view, interest, by its very nature produces selfishness, cruelty, hard-heartiness, money-worship etc., and kills the spirit of co-operation. It is therefore, ruinous to the society both morally and economically. As to the question: What should one do with the money for which one has no use, one may invest it in commerce, industry, etc., on the basis of partnership and share profits and losses alike.

This allowance applies only to the legal aspect of that interest which had been taken before the revelation of this verse about prohibition and does not mean that the income from that interest had also been made lawful. From the very wording of the verse, it is clear that the case will go to Allah for judgement and that it has not been pardoned outright by Allah. In order to avoid endless litigation on this account, it has been asserted that no legal demand for its return should be made. But from the moral point of view, it remains unclean and one who has taken it must do his best to cleanse himself of it. He should abstain from squandering it on himself and try his best to find out the people from whom he received it and return it to them. In case he is unable to locate or find anyone of those people, he should spend the unclean and unlawful wealth on social welfare. This is the only way he can save himself from the punishment of Allah,

Who will decide the case on the Day of Judgement. As to the person who goes on lavishing unlawful wealth, he may be liable to punishment even for his money lending in the past.

From the social point of view, even a little thinking will show that a society can never become strong and stable if its members found their mutual feelings on selfishness and if one is willing to help the other without self –interest. If the rich people think that the poor people exist merely to afford them an opportunity for exploitation, there will be a clash of interests which will result in the disintegration of that society. If other factors also help this evil state of affairs, these will surely produce a class struggle. On the other hand, if the individual members of the society base their dealings on mutual sympathy and treat each other with generosity, they will surely make it stronger. If everyone tries to help the other in need, and if the "haves" treat the "have-nots" with sympathy or at least with justice and mutual love will evolve in the society and it will become strong and stable.

As for the fixed interest on economic loans, three of the many evils are given below:

1. Those concerns that cannot pay an interest higher than or equal to the market rate cannot draw in capital. All the available money into those channels of commerce and industry which can bring interest equal to or greater than the market rate of interest, however damaging they might be from the national point of view.

2. There is no business, commercial, industrial, agricultural, that can guarantee a fixed or uniform rate of profit, say five, six or ten per cent or more under all conditions. Not to speak of such a guarantee, there cannot be a guarantee against loss in any business.

3. As the money-lender himself is not immediately a partner in the profit and loss of the business but keeps in sight only his guaranteed fixed interest, he is not interested in its welfare. His only concern is his own interest. He very selfishly tries to withdraw and withhold his money whenever he has even the slightest apprehension of a slump in the market. In this way he produces panic by his selfishness and paves the way for a further crisis and when there is already a crisis, he speeds it into a disaster.

This verse was revealed after the conquest of Makkah, but it has been placed here because it also deals with interest. Even before its revelation, interest was considered as a hateful thing in the Muslim society, though it had not yet been affirmed to be unlawful. But after the revelation, money-lending at interest became a criminal offence in the Islamic State. Those clans who transmitted business in Arabia, were duly warned to give up this business, or otherwise a war would be declared against them. When the Christians of Najran were granted autonomy, with the Islamic State, it was specified in the treaty that if they continued the practice there would be a state of war between the two.

From the concluding portion of this verse, Ibn 'Abbas, Hasan Basri, Ibn Sarin and Rubai bin Anas have deduced that the one who takes interest in the Islamic State should be warned to repent of it, and if even then he does not give it up, he should be put to death. But the other jurists are of the opinion that he should be put in prison and detained there until he undertakes to give up his business.

This verse enables the Islamic court of law to force the creditors to give more time to the debtors for the payment of debts, if they are in such straightened circumstances that they cannot pay back their debts. Under certain circumstances, the court is entitled to write off all or a part of it. A tradition says that a man suffered loss in his business and came heavily under debt. When his case was taken to the Holy Prophet, he made an appeal to the people to help him out of it. Accordingly, the people made monetary contributions, but he could not even then clear all of his debts. Then the Holy Prophet addressed the creditors and told them they would have to be satisfied with whatever was collected for the payment of their debts.

Ar Rum :39

This is the first verse revealed in the Qur'an that condemned interest. It only says this. You pay interest thinking that it will cause an increase in the wealth of the money-lender, but actually, in the sight of Allah, interest does not increase the wealth, but the wealth is increased by the payment of the "Zakat". Afterwards when the Commandment prohibiting interest was revealed at Medinah, it was said, "Allah deprives interest of all blessing and develops charity."

This verse has been given two interpretations by the commentators. One section of them says: Here riba, does not mean the interest which is forbidden by the Shariah but it means the gift or the present which is given with the purpose that the recipient will return it redoubled, or will discharge some useful service for the donor, or his becoming prosperous will be beneficial for the donor himself. This is the view of Ibn 'Abbas, Mujahid, Dahjak, Qatadah, 'Ikrimah, Muhammad bin Ka'b al-Qursi and Sha'bi. Probably this remark has been made by these scholars for the reason that in this verse the only consequence mentioned of the act is that in the sight of Allah such wealth will not increase at all, if, however, it had been meant the interest forbidden by the Shariah it would have been positively said that it would have been rigidly punished by Allah.

The other group differs from this and says that it means the same well known riba' which has been forbidden by the Shariah. This is the opinion of Hasan Basri and Suddi, 'Allama Alus also has opined that the apparent meaning of the verse is the same, for riba' in Arabic is used in the same meaning. This interpretation has been adopted by the commentator Nisabor also.

In our opinion also this second interpretation is correct, for the argument given in favor of the first interpretation is not enough for discarding the known meaning of the word riba'. In the period when Surah Ar-Rum was sent down. Interest had not been forbidden yet.

95

The prohibition was made several years afterwards. The way of the Qur'an is that it first prepares the minds for the thing that it has to prohibit at a later stage. About wine also the only thing said in the beginning was that it was not pure food. (An-Nahl: 67). Then in Al-Baqarah: 219, it was said that the harm of its sin is greater than its benefit. Then it was enjoined that the Prayer should not be offered in the state of intoxication. (An-Nisa':43). Then, finally, it was prohibited totally. Similarly, about interest here it has been only said that it does not increase the wealth, but the real increase is caused by the Zakat. After this, the compound interest was forbidden. (Al-i-Imran:130); and finally, interest itself was made absolutely unlawful. (Al-Baqarah:275).

Al-I-Imran :130

The main cause of the setback at Uhud was the selfishness for wealth shown by the Muslims. They were so overwhelmed by lust for booty, that, instead of chasing their initial success to victory, they got engaged in plundering the spoils. This is why the All-Wise Allah has struck at interest, the root cause of the evils and prohibited it. For a common experience that those who lend money on interest become so preoccupied in it, that day and night they think of nothing but increasing their unearned profits and this naturally increasing their greed for money.

The gorging of interest had created greed and selfishness in those who took interest and hatred, anger, enmity, and jealousy in those who had to pay it, and those moral evils contributed to some extent to the setback in the Battle of Uhud. Allah has condemned and prohibited interest and prescribed charity as an antidote to it. It is obvious that Paradise has been reserved for those who practice charity and spend money unstinting, and not for those greedy persons who practice money on interest.

Islam is not mere words one utters, but a comprehensive and system of life. To deny a part of it is to reject it all. In this case, there is not the slightest doubt that *riba* is totally forbidden. Hence, to legalize it and build the life of society on it is a grave offence.

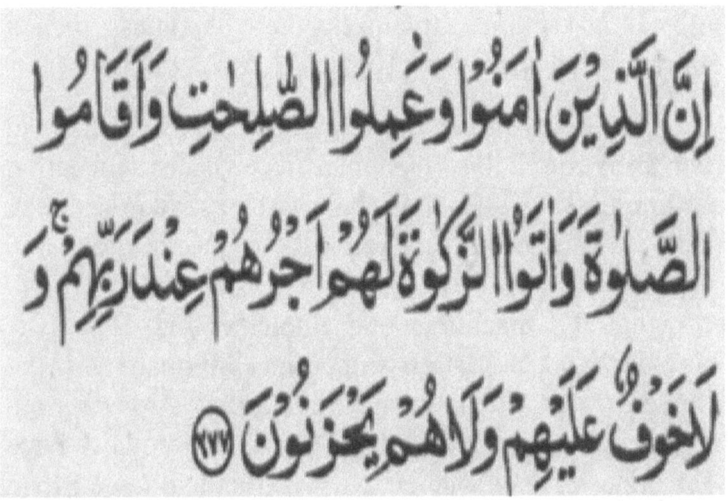

It says:

Those that have faith and do good deeds, attend regularly to their Prayers and give zakat, shall have their reward with their Lord. They shall have nothing to fear nor shall they grieve. **Qur'an (al Bakarah) 2:277**

The main element of this verse is that of *zakat* which denotes donating willingly, expecting nothing from any human being in return. The verse also introduces a feature of the community of believers and one of its important pillars, before it goes on to depict

98

the total reassurance, tranquility and happiness such a community enjoys.

God also makes it a condition that Muslims, in order to be true believers, should receive this legislation and implement it in their daily life as soon as they become aware of it. The surah also stresses fear and consciousness of God as a necessary corollary to following His teachings and implementing His laws. This fear of God is an important safeguard for the enforcement of the laws and regulations strengthening the guarantees inherent in them. Thus, Islamic laws have a far better chance of being obeyed and followed than man made laws. The enforcement of the latter is solely contingent on the force of external authority which is easily evaded and circumvented in the absence of the inner incentives and convictions of a vigilant conscience.

The alternative is far gloomy. "If you do not, then war is declared against you by God and his Messenger. If you repent, however, you shall remain entitled to your principle. Thus, you shall commit no wrong, nor suffer any wrong yourselves." What a terrifying prospect! How could the frail and powerless humans even consider going to war against God and His Messenger. The outcome is a foregone conclusion.

The war that God and his Messenger are ready to conduct against the perpetrators of *riba* is much wider in concept than the use of armed forces by a worldly ruler. It is a warning of a total condemnation of all societies adopting *riba* as a basis for their social and economic life. It is a war effecting the psychological, economic and emotional aspects of life. It is the social strife and antagonism brought about by the exploitive *riba* system, as well as the regional and international conflict and instability tolerated in consequence by all humanity. It is a war initiated, directly or indirectly, by moneylenders and international capitalists who, like sharks, prey on corporations, businesses, industries, commerce, governments and states. Their predatory activities are the root cause of run-a-way inflation, high taxation, crippling international debts, recessions and poverty. All of which are able of starting wars and fueling bloodshed and destruction all over the world. The outcome of this vicious cycle of misery is economic deprivation, moral degradation, social disintegration and the inevitable collapse of human civilization.

Salvage of the principle capital in commercial dealings cannot be said to be inequitable to either lender or borrower. There are countless legitimate ways and means for investment, growth and development of capital, employing one's own entrepreneurial skills or by working in partnership with others, in which all parties proportionally share in the loss and profit of the enterprise. These would include many profitable and equitable forms of business such as trading in shares of companies whose profits are justly distributed among the share-holders, cooperative banks that invest in commercial and industrial projects and distributes profits (and losses) among depositors, rather than give a fixed rate return on deposits. Such banks would be entitled to price appropriate service or management fees.

The surah concludes with lending and borrowing with advice related to bankrupt debtors. In such cases, the solution would not be to impose further penalties in lieu of deferred payment, but the debtor should be granted a reprieve until he is able to settle his debt, or the lender should be magnanimous enough to write off the debt completely.

If the debtor is in stressful circumstances, alloy him a delay until a time of ease. And if you waive (the debt entirely) as a gift of charity, it will be better for you, if you but knew it (2: 280).

The words evoke an atmosphere of tolerance and benevolence and provide a respite from the harshness and severity of greed and selfishness. They call for leniency and sympathy on the part of the creditor and the borrower, as well as by society as a whole.

Then, in a highly inspiring comment, the *surah* recalls the fearful Day of Judgement when people shall stand defenseless before God to explain for their actions. These words cannot fail to move a caring and conscientious person to write off any money he might be owed by some helpless borrower.

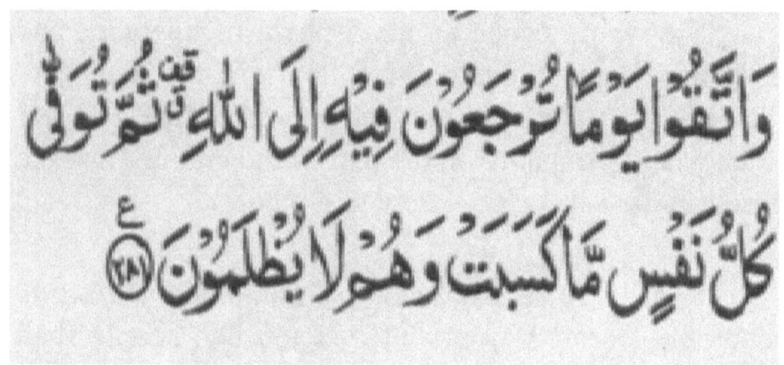

Fear the day when you all shall return to God; when every soul shall be repaid in full for what it had earned and none shall be wronged.   *Qur'an (al Bakarah)2: 281*

This fear is that powerful "voice within" which Islam kindles in the deepest recess of people's minds and hearts to act as a potent guiding force in life. Islam proves yet again how vigorous, well-integrated, practical and merciful it is, and confirms that its overriding aim and objective is the happiness and wellbeing of man as an individual and of human society as a whole.

Usury: The Way to Inevitable Ruin

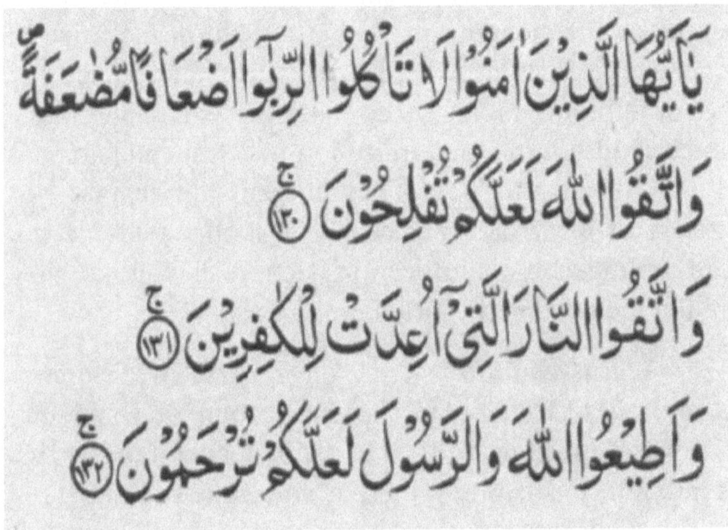

Believers, do not gorge yourselves on usury, doubling (your money) again and again. Have fear of God, so that you may prosper. Guard yourselves against the Fire which has been prepared for the unbelievers; and obey God and the messenger, that you may be graced with mercy.

Qur'an (al li Imran)3:130-132

Here we will only briefly comment on the multiplication of the principle sum of a loan. Some people in our modern times want to control the verse in order to make lawful what God has forbidden. They say the prohibition is restricted only to excessive usury which guides to the multiplication of a principle amount of money time after time. They further claim that rates of interest of 4,5,7 or 9 per cent and similar rates do not lead to any such multiplication. Hence, they argue, they are not included in the prohibition of usury.

Let us begin by stating clearly that the reference to multiples is simply a characterization of something that was happening in life. It is not a condition for the prohibition to operate. The Qur'anic statement in surah 2, The Cow, makes a clear prohibition of all usury. It addresses the believers and bids them *"give up what remains outstanding of usury."* (2:278) It applies to all that exceeds the principle amount, without qualification.

It is impossible in any case for faith and usury to exist side by side. Wherever usury is adopted as a system the faith of Islam, as a whole, does not exist. There can only be the fire which has been prepared for the unbelievers. Any debate against this is simply futile. The fact that these verses combine the express probation of usury with calling on believers to fear God and guard against the Fire is not a mere chance. It is made in order to establish this fact clearly in the minds of Muslims. It is also made in the hope of achieving prosperity through renouncing usury and maintaining fear of God. For prosperity is the natural outcome of fearing God and implementing the Devine method in human life. We have only to warn ourselves of these catastrophic effects in order to recognize the meaning of prosperity in this context, and the fact that it is made conditional on abandoning this hateful system.

Surah Al-Rum (30)

Since it is God who grants provisions and sustenance, giving in abundance and small measure as He pleases, He designates to people a way in which they can make handsome a profit, enlarging their wealth. This is different from what they think:

106

فَـَٔاتِ ذَا الْقُرْبَىٰ حَقَّهُۥ وَالْمِسْكِينَ وَابْنَ السَّبِيلِ ذَٰلِكَ خَيْرٌ لِّلَّذِينَ يُرِيدُونَ وَجْهَ اللَّهِ وَأُوْلَٰٓئِكَ هُمُ الْمُفْلِحُونَ ۝ وَمَآ ءَاتَيْتُم مِّن رِّبًا لِّيَرْبُوَا۟ فِىٓ أَمْوَٰلِ النَّاسِ فَلَا يَرْبُوا۟ عِندَ اللَّهِ وَمَآ ءَاتَيْتُم مِّن زَكَوٰةٍ تُرِيدُونَ وَجْهَ اللَّهِ فَأُوْلَٰٓئِكَ هُمُ الْمُضْعِفُونَ ۝

Hence, give his due to the near of kin, as well as to the needy and the traveler in need. This is best for all who seek God's countenance. It is they who shall be successful. Whatever you may give out in usury so that it might increase through other people's property will bring no increase with God, whereas all that you give out in charity, seeking God's countenance, will bring you multiple increase.

Qur'an (Al Rum) 30: 38-39

Since all wealth belongs to God, and it is He who grants it to some of His servants, He, the original owner, has ascertained that a portion of it should go to certain groups, to be given to them by those who are in actual possession of it. Therefore, He calls it a right due to these groups, of which the surah mentions here *"the near of kin, the needy and the traveler in need."* At the time this surah was revealed, zakat had not yet been determined, nor its beneficiaries. The principle, however, is stated clearly, making all money God's property since it is, He who grants it in the first place, and allocated it to certain needy groups a right which they should receive from those who are in possession of the money. This is the basic financial principle Islam lays down, from which all aspects of the Islamic economic theory derive. Since all money and wealth belong to God, it is subject to what He, as the original owner, determines with regard to how it is owned, invested or spent. The person who is control of it does not enjoy absolute authority in this   respect.

God Almighty issues this directive to those He has placed as trustees of wealth showing them the best methods for investments, growth and prosperity. This means sharing with one's near kin, the needy and stranded travelers, and spending regularly in ways that serve God's cause, *"This is best for all who seek God's countenance. It is they who shall be successful."* (Verse 38)

SELECTED BIBLIOGRAPHY OF BOOKS AND SUGGESTED READING

Brown, Ellen Hodgson, The Web of Debt (Third Millennium Press, 2008).

Griffin, G. Edward, The Creature from Jekyll Island (Westlake Village, California: American Media, 1998).

Guttman, Robert, How Credit-Money Shapes the Economy (Armonk, New. E. Sharpe, 1994).

Khan, Adnan, The Global Credit Crunch and the Crisis of Capitalism (www.khilafah.com,June 2008).

Perkins, John, Confessions of an Economic Hit Man (San Francisco: Berrett-Koehler Publishers, Inc., 2004).

Qutb, Sayyid, IN THE SHADE OF THE QURAN (MWH London Publishers,1979).

Yusuf Ali, Abdullah, (translator), The Holy Quran (Published by Amana Corp. 4411 41st St. Brentwood, Maryland 20722, 1983).

Articles

Wright Patman, <u>A Primer on Money</u> (Government Printing Office, prepared for the Sub-committee on Domestic Finance, House of Representatives, Committee on Banking and Currency, 88th Congress, 2nd session, 1964), chapter 3.

Chicago Federal Reserve, <u>Modern Money Mechanics</u> (1963), originally produced and distributed free by the Public Information Center of the Federal Reserve Bank of Chicago, Chicago Illinois, now available on the internet at http//landru.i-link-2net/monques/mmm2.html.

Christopher White, Testimony Submitted on April 13, 1994 to the House Committee on Banking, Finance and Urban Affairs, "The Monetary System Is Collapsing," <u>The New Federalist</u> (May 30, 1994).

Ellen Brown, "Behind the Drums of War with Iran: Nuclear Weapons or Compound Interest? ", webdebt.com/articles (November 13,2007); "Why is Iran Still in the Cross-Hairs? Clues from the Project for a New American Century," <u>ibid</u> (January 9, 2007).

IMF Research Department Staff, "Capital Flow Sustainability and Speculative Currency Attacks," worldbank.org (November 12, 1997).

Bill Murphy, "Moral Hazard," LeMetropoleCafe.com (September 8, 2006), reposted at gata.org/node/4361

(September 9, 2006), quoting Joe Stocks at siliconinvestor.com/readmsg.aspx?msgid=22789705.

Containing System Risks and restoring Financial Soundness, Global financial stability report, IMF, April 2008, http://imf.org/external/pubs/ft/gfsr/2008/01/pdf/text.pdf

Bank of England statistical release, M0 December 2007

Federal Reserve Statistical release 2006

Bank for international settlements, Monetary and Economic Department, Triennial Central Bank, *Survey of Foreign Exchange and Derivatives Market Activity in April 2007'* Preliminary global results, September 2007, Switzerland, http://www.bis.org/publ/rpfx07.pdf?noframes=1

Paul Krugman, MIT Professor of Economics, Princeton University, How Washington Worsened Asia's Crash: The Confidence Game, http the new republic.com/archive/1098/100598/krugman100598.html and http://web.mit.edu/krugman/www/myth.html

2005 Economic, Survey, income data, US Census Bureau,

Glossary

Bank 'run': A type of financial crisis where panic leads to a large number of customers of a bank to withdraw their deposits because they fear that it is, or may become insolvent. Because banks retain only a fraction of their deposits as cash the remainder is invested in securities and loans. No bank has enough reserves on hand to cope with more than a fraction of the deposits being taken out at once. As a result, the bank faces bankruptcy, and will 'call in' the loans it has offered.

Collateral: A security or guarantee (usually an asset) pledged for the repayment of a loan if one cannot repay the debt.

Credit crunch: A credit crunch is a sudden reduction in the availability of loans (or credit) or a sudden increase in the cost of obtaining a loan from banks.

Credit Rating: A credit rating assesses the credit worthiness of an individual, corporation, or even a country. Credit ratings are calculated from financial history and current assets and liabilities. Typically, a credit rating undertaken by a credit rating agency tells a lender or investor the probability of the subject being able to pay back a loan.

Deregulation :A term which gained widespread currency in the 1970-2000, it is where governments remove, reduce, or simplify rules in the sectors that make up the economy. The stated rational for deregulation is that fewer and simpler regulations will lead to a raised level of competitiveness, therefore higher productivity, more efficiency and lower prices overall.

Default : This occurs when a debtor has not met his legal obligations according to the debt contract, e.g. it has not made a scheduled payment, or has violated a loan condition of the debt contract.

Derivatives :Financial instruments whose value changes in response to values in underlying variables. The main type of derivatives are futures, forwards, options, and swaps.

Financial markets : A financial market is a mechanism that allows people to easily buy and sell (trade) financial securities (such as stocks and bonds), commodities such as precious metals or agricultural goods.

Fractional reserve banking : A banking practice in which banks keep only a fraction of their deposits in reserve with the choice of lending out remainder while maintain the obligation to redeem all deposits on demand.

Government intervention : Actions taken by government within the economy to deal with market failure or imbalances which generally are left to markets.

Hedge fund: A private investment fund that charges a performance fee and is typically open to a limited range of qualified investors. Hedge fund activity in the financial markets has grown substantially and constitutes 30% of all fixed-income security transactions, 55% of activity in derivatives with investment-grade ratings, 55% of trading volume for emerging-market bonds, as well as 30% of equity trades. Total industry assets reached $2.68 trillion in 2007.

Inflation : A sustained increase in the general level of prices, which is equivalent to a decline in the value or purchasing power of money. If the supply of money and credit increases too rapidly over many months, the result will be inflation.

Liquidity : An asset's ability to be easily converted through an act of buying or selling without causing a significant movement in the price and with minimum loss of value. A liquid asset is considered one that can be sold rapidly, with minimal loss of value and anytime within market hours.

Moral Hazard : The prospect that a party insulated from risk may behave differently than it would behave if it were fully exposed to the risk.

NASDAQ : The National Association of Securities Dealers Automated Quotation System is an American stock exchange with the electronic screen-based equity securities trading market in the United States. With approximately 3,200, it lists more companies and has more trades per day than any other US market.

Nationalization : The act of taking an industry or assets into the public ownership of a national government.

Remortgaging : Or Re-financing is the process of paying off one mortgage with the proceeds from a new mortgage using the same property as security.

Recession : The opposite of economic growth – where the economy shrinks. A country is considered to be in a recession when its economy shrinks for two consecutive quarters.

Risk : The probability that an investment's actual return will be different than expected. This includes the possibility of losing some of or all of the original investment. It is usually measured by calculating the standard deviation of the historical returns or average returns of a specific investment.

Securitization: A finance process where assets, receivables or financial instruments are acquired, classified into pools and offered as collateral for further borrowing. Due to securitization, risky loans can be packaged with less risky loans in affect making the whole instrument investment grade

Short Selling : The practice of selling securities the seller does not own, in the hope of repurchasing them later at a lower price. This is done to profit from a decline in price of a security, such as a share of a bond. In contrast ordinarily one would 'go along' purchasing a security hoping the price will rise.

Speculative attack: Actions undertaken by speculators involving the massive selling of a currency. This has much in common with cornering the market, as it involves building up a large directional position in the hope of exiting at a better price. As such, relies entirely on the market reacting to the attack by continuing the move that has been engineered, in order for profits to be made by the attackers.

Solvency : A financial condition experienced by a person or business entity when their assets exceed their liabilities. A company is considered to be insolvent if its liabilities exceed its assets because it can no longer meet its debt obligations when they come due.

Stock market : A market where shares are bought and sold

Treasury bonds : A debt security, in which the authorized issuer owes the holders a debt and is obliged to repay the principle and interest (the coupon) at a later date, termed maturity. Treasury bonds are the US government bonds issued by the United States Department of the Treasury through the Bureau of the Public Debt. T-Bonds, or the long bond have the longest maturity, from ten years to thirty years.

Tiger economies : The 'tiger' economy was a term coined to describe South Korea, Singapore, Hong Kong, and Taiwan who underwent rapid growth and industrialization in the 1960's and 1970's. The four tigers share a range of characteristics with other Asian economies, such as China and Japan, and pioneered what has become to be seen as a particularly "Asian" approach to economic development, that of an export driven economy.

Venture capital : A type of private equity capital typically provided by professional, outside investors to new startups. Typically, money is made from the new start up profits rather than share price rises.